To my friends Elida Saucedo and Darby McQuade,
to my cousins Ada Paulina and Hernan Díaz Batista, Manuel Garcia Hernandez,
Genoveva Rosales Lopez and her family and friends in Oaxaca,
to Herminio Martínez Matías and his family in Teotitlan del Valle,
and to the family who let me enter their lives and adopted me: Samuel Montaño
Chavez, Refugio Ruíz Jimenez, Rigel, Shaula, Cristina, and Angelita Montaño Ruíz—

Gracias

Other books that give information about *el Día de Los Muertos* include
The Days of the Dead. Greenleigh and Beimler.
San Francisco: Collins, 1991.
The Skeleton at the Feast. Carmichael and Sayer.
Austin: University of Texas Press, 1992.
Vive tu Recuerdo. Childs and Altman. Los Angeles:
University of California Press, 1982.

First Edition   2 3 4 5 6 7 8 9 10

Library of Congress Cataloging in Publication

Ancona, George. Pablo remembers: the Fiesta of the Day of the Dead / by George Ancona.
p.   cm.   Summary: During the three-day celebration of the Day of the Dead, a young Mexican boy and his family make
elaborate preparations to honor the spirits of the dead.   ISBN 0-688-11249-8. —ISBN 0-688-11250-1 (lib. bdg.).
—ISBN 0-688-12894-7 (Spanish Language Edition) 1. Mexico—Social life and customs—Juvenile literature.
2. All Souls' Day—Mexico—Juvenile literature.   [1. All Souls' Day—Mexico.   2. Mexico—Social life and customs.]
1. Title. F1210.A75   1993   393'.9'0972—dc20   92-22819   CIP   AC

PABLO REMEMBERS

❖ The Fiesta of the Day of the Dead ❖

George Ancona

LOTHROP, LEE & SHEPARD BOOKS ◆ NEW YORK

for Genoveva

All Hallows Eve

The village church bells are ringing and the rooster is crowing. Pablo knows it is time to get up. The first thing he sees when he opens his eyes is the picture of Abuelita, his grandmother. The smiling photograph on his wall, made when she was a young mother, is the only one that was ever taken of her. Pablito remembers her with white hair and wrinkled hands—but the very same smile. Abuelita died two years ago, and he misses her.

Today, the three-day *fiesta* of *el Día de Los Muertos*, the Day of the Dead, begins — a time when Abuelita seems especially close. Everyone has so much to do to get ready. Pablo can hear his mother, Señora Refugio, already bustling about in the kitchen.

"*Niños*, hurry and get dressed," she calls, "or we'll miss the bus."

Usually when Pablo is not in school, he is working alongside his father, Señor Samuel, weaving the beautiful rugs that have made their village famous. But today there is no school, and there is no time for weaving, either. Today Pablo and his sister Shaula are going to help their parents shop in the big city market of Oaxaca. Their two younger sisters, Cristina and Angelita, will stay behind with their godmother.

People everywhere in México are busy preparing for the *fiesta,* the holiday. Bakers are baking the traditional *pan de muertos,* the bread of the dead. Candy makers are making sugar skulls. Children are cutting out cardboard skeletons. Artisans are stamping out tissue-paper decorations called *estampas.* Farmers are harvesting *cempasúchil,* marigolds, the flowers of the dead.

The Oaxaca market is already crowded when Pablo, Shaula, and their parents arrive. As they make their way through the throng, the children watch their parents examine the fruits, taste the nuts, and bargain with the vendors for the best prices. They buy:

NARANJAS *(oranges)*
MANZANAS *(apples)*
CHILES *(peppers)*
NUECES Y CACAHUATES *(pecans and peanuts)*
CHAPULINES *(fried grasshoppers)*
CACAO *(cocoa beans)*

CALABAZA

❧❖❧

(pumpkin)

COPAL

❧❖❧

(a resin incense)

Cal
❧❖❧
(lime)

Pan de Muertos
❧❖❧
(bread of the dead)

VELAS *(candles)*

TOMATES Y JITOMATES *(tomatoes)*

CAÑA *(sugarcane)*

LIMONES *(lemons)*

RÁBANOS *(radishes)*

ESPECIAS *(spices)*

CEMPASÚCHIL *(marigolds)*

CALAVERAS DE DULCE *(sugar skulls)*

At last they have everything they need. Loaded down with packages, they catch the bus for their village.

Back home, Pablo, Shaula, Cristina, and Angelita make a children's altar. The altar will invite the *angelitos*, spirits of dead children, to come back for a visit tonight. Everything on it is small. The children fill small baskets with nuts. They pour *chocolate*, hot cocoa, into small cups. They place sugar skulls decorated with their own names on the altar. Pablo lights the copal incense, and its smoke fills the room with its perfume. Flowers and fruits and toys complete their *ofrenda*, or offering, to the little spirits. Finally Pablo lights the *velita*, the small candle to light the way for the *angelitos*. It will burn all night long.

By the time they have finished making their altar, it is time to go to bed. As Pablito falls asleep, he hears his mother, still busy in the kitchen. She will be up late into the night, cooking the chicken, soaking and cooking corn kernels in lime, and making all the other preparations for the day ahead.

The next morning, Señora Refugio prepares an early breakfast for the family. The children dip their *pan de muertos* into steaming cups of *chocolate*. *Atole* is a treat for everyone, a warm drink made from ground corn that has been cooked in water. Then comes chicken broth served with large tortillas called *tlalludas*—a hearty beginning to this special day.

Everyone has plenty of chores to do after breakfast. They must clean the house and have all the food ready by three o'clock, when family will begin to arrive. By then the *angelitos* will be ready to depart, and the adult spirits will come to visit. Pablo fetches water for his mother and cleans the yard. Shaula washes the dishes while Cristina and Angelita feed cornmeal to the chickens and turkeys.

Señora Refugio begins to prepare the traditional meal for the festival, *tamales de mole*. First she drains the lime water from the softened corn. She takes the kernels to a neighbor's mill, and the miller grinds it into a coarse dough.

Señora Refugio kneels beside her *metate* to grind the *chocolate, chiles,* and *especias* for her mole sauce. Stone *metates* have been used for centuries to grind food.

While the señora dices the chicken she cooked last night, Shaula begins to make the *tortillas*. Using a little machine called a *tortilladora*, she presses the corn dough into small, flat circles.

Working together, the girls and their mother make the *tamales*. They cover each *tortilla* with mole sauce and chicken. Then they fold it, wrap it in corn husks, and tie it. When they have prepared all the *tamales*, Señora Refugio steams them in a large pot, and the wonderful smell of *tamales de mole* fills the air.

Meanwhile, Pablo and his father have gone to the local market to buy some last-minute things for the grown-ups' *ofrenda*. They waited till midday so that the flowers for the altar would be fresh. They also buy long sugarcanes with which to build an arch.

It is nearly three o'clock — time is running out. Pablito and Señor Samuel hurry home. When they arrive, Señor Samuel calls everyone to come help finish building the large altar.

Señora Refugio spreads a cloth on a table and centers a crucifix on it. Then the children and their parents pile the table high with *pan de muertos, frutas* (fruits), *flores* (flowers), cups of *chocolate* and *atole,* and special things that their dead relatives enjoyed during their lifetime—their favorite foods, candies, or drinks. When the *tamales* are cooked, some will be placed on the *ofrenda* as well.

Señora Refugio lights the wick in the bowl of lamp oil in front of the crucifix. There is also a candle for each of the relatives.

Finally, they place photographs of their dead relatives on the altar. "Now Abuelita can come to visit," says Shaula.

Just as the altar is ready, the sounds of fireworks fill the air. That is the signal that the spirits of the dead are on their way home. For the next twenty-four hours, the church bells will toll continuously. Teams of young men will take turns ringing them.

"And now we can eat!" shouts Pablo. The smell of cooking *tamales* has been teasing his appetite all this time. Señora Refugio uncovers the steaming pot and fills a basket with *tamales* for the children. Their parents will eat later with the guests.

After they have eaten, Pablito and his sisters put on their new clothes—the first guests will arrive any minute. The visiting will go on late into the night and again the next day. Aunts, uncles, cousins, grandparents, godmothers, and godfathers will all come. Each family will bring a *canasta* filled with pumpkin candy, flowers, and candles to place on the altar. They will stay awhile to visit. Then they will fill their empty baskets with some of the food from the altar and go on to the next relative's house.

In between receiving guests, Pablo's family also goes visiting, and Pablo runs off to play with some of his friends. It is a day filled with feasting and talk and play and laughter for everyone, and the *fiesta* goes on even after Pablo can no longer keep his eyes open.

All Souls Day

The next morning, some of the villagers attend the church, which is decorated with tall candles, flowers, and offerings of food.

This is the day when families go to the cemetery to decorate the graves and tombs of their relatives. The flowers for the graves must be fresh, so Señora Refugio makes one last trip to the market. She is too late to buy more purple cockscomb, but she manages to find some *cempasúchil*.

At three o'clock, the bells stop ringing. A burst of fireworks erupts, signaling the departure of the spirits.

Now Pablo and his family gather up flowers and a picnic and join all the other village families in the cemetery. Señor Samuel sweeps the area around the family tombs. Pablo helps his mother decorate the graves with flowers and fruits. Then the family sits together, eating, singing, laughing, and keeping their dead relatives company. Neighbors come and go, sharing in the celebration.

The children play games around the tombs. One of Angelita's favorites is played with a coin and walnuts. The children poke the coin into the ground, and each one tries to hit it with a nut. The nuts that miss remain on the ground until one of the children hits the coin. That child wins and gets to keep all the nuts.

As dusk falls, Pablito lights the candles on Abuelita's tomb. Gradually the sky turns black, the stars twinkle, and a quiet descends on the cemetery. In the flickering candlelight, people sit and think, remembering the loved ones who are buried there.

Pablo turns to Shaula. "I think Abuelita is happy that we are all here with her tonight," he says. Shaula smiles and nods.

As the grownups chat, Cristina and Angelita snuggle into their parents' arms. Their eyes begin to droop. Soon they will all go home to a hot cup of *chocolate* and a warm bed.

They have spent the last three days celebrating their ancestors. For Pablo, being with Abuelita has been the most special of all. Pablito knows he will always remember her. And as the years pass, he will celebrate her memory again and again on *el Día de Los Muertos.*

A Note from the Author

The celebration of the Day of the Dead grew from the blending of Aztec beliefs about death with Catholic beliefs that the Spanish conquistadors brought to the people of México.

The ancient Egyptians thought that the spirits of the dead returned in the autumn to visit the world of the living. They welcomed these spirits with food and lights. These customs spread to ancient Rome, and when Christianity was born, the remembrance of the dead was adopted. In time, November 1 became All Hallows or All Saints day, a day to pray for the innocent souls of saints and martyrs and children. By the thirteenth century, the following day, All Souls Day, was set aside to remember the spirits of sinners who had died. October 31 at some point became All Hallows Eve, when the spirits of dead children came to visit. They left the next day, when adult spirits arrived. In Spain, these days were celebrated by placing food and candles on the family graves in churches and cemeteries.

On the other side of the globe, the Aztecs, Maya, and other pre-Hispanic peoples saw death as a part of the process of life. A person's afterlife depended on how he or she died. For example, warriors went to accompany the sun god, Tonatiuh, and after four years became hummingbirds and butterflies. Infants went to Chichihuacuahco, where they were nursed by milk-sweating trees.

The Aztecs believed that at the end of the present world, everyone who had died would be born again. They honored the spirits of the dead and invited them to visit on certain days of the year. On those days, they placed offerings of *tamales* and *atole* on tombs. Extra *tamales* were offered to neighbors. When the Spanish conquered Mexico and forced its people to become Christian, it wasn't very difficult for the Aztecs to adapt their own rites to Catholic ceremonies.

Today the festival of the Day of the Dead is mainly a family celebration, a reunion of the living with their dead relatives. Every community celebrates in its own way. In some villages a *comparsa*, or masquerade, takes place one night. Men, women, and children dress up in costumes and masks and parade behind a band. These mummers stop at some houses to recite funny verses about their neighbors. Some towns light candles in the cemeteries one night but not the other.

José Guadalupe Posada was a nineteenth-century artist who is remembered for his woodcuts making fun of Mexican society and showing people as skeletons. Today his work inspires artists to create altars using his images in museums and public buildings. These *ofrendas* often honor famous artists, writers, and public figures who have died.

Mexican communities in the United States also celebrate the Day of the Dead, blending their traditional *fiesta* with the American Halloween.

To Mexicans, the *fiesta* of the Day of the Dead is both a public holiday and a private one. Publicly, the community makes light of death and pokes fun at it. Privately, people honor the memories of their deceased family members.

Glossary of Spanish Words

abuelita — diminutive of *abuela* (grandmother); diminutives are used as terms of endearment

angelito — little angel or spirit

atole — a gruel drink prepared with cornmeal

canasta — a basket or hamper

chiles — all varieties of red, green, and yellow peppers

chocolate — cacao, sugar, cinnamon, and nuts, ground and made into a chocolate wafer; also, a hot cocoa drink

comparsa — a costumed parade

copal — a type of resin used as incense

estampa — a die-cut tissue-paper design

fiesta — a feast or festival, a holy day

flores — flowers

frutas — fruits

gracias — thank you

metate — a stone with a concave upper surface, used for grinding seeds, vegetables, etc.

mole — a fricassee made with chiles, spices, and often with ground cocoa

niños — children

Oaxaca — a state and city in southern Mexico

ofrenda — an offering or gift; also, an altar with offerings and decorations on it

Pablito — diminutive of Pablo

pan de muertos — bread of the dead

señor — Mr.; also, a gentleman

señora — Mrs.; also, a lady

tamale — a dish made by placing a filling in dough which is then wrapped in banana leaves or softened corn husks and steamed

tamales de mole — tamales made with mole sauce

tortilla — a thin, round, unleavened pancake made with cornmeal or sometimes wheat flour

tortillador — a press used in making tortillas

tlalluda — a large tortilla

velita — a small candle